22/5/12

GRASS GROWS BY ITSELF

ELIZABETH CAIN

GRASS GROWS BY ITSELF

MEDITATING GENTLY FOR SELF-ACCEPTANCE

MILLENNIUM BOOKS

First published by
Millennium Books
an imprint of E. J. Dwyer (Australia) Pty Ltd
Unit 13
Perry Park
33 Maddox Street
Alexandria NSW 2015
Australia
Phone: (02) 550-2355
Fax: (02) 519-3218

Distributed in the U.S.A. by Seven Hills Book Distributors
49 Central Avenue
Cincinnati OH 45202

National Library of Australia
Cataloguing-in-Publication data

Cain, Elizabeth, 1935- .
  Grass grows by itself.

  ISBN 1 86429 009 9.

  1. Meditation. 2. Meditations. I. Title.

158.12

Cover design by NB Design
Text design by NB Design
Art by Mark Dixon
Typeset in 11½ on 13½pt Baskerville by Post Typesetters
Printed by Australian Print Group, Maryborough, Vic.

10 9 8 7 6 5 4 3 2 1
99, 98, 97 96 95

Grass Grows By Itself may be read in a leisurely way, pondered, and perhaps extended in some form of active meditation. It may be used at any time, by oneself, with a spiritual companion, or in a group. It aims to accompany and facilitate the wonder of spiritual unfoldment. Repetitions are deliberate. They are ways of returning to earlier places, of deepening them and opening them out.

Dedication

Grass Grows By Itself
is dedicated to each of my companions on the journey.

Acknowledgment

My thanks to the Coragulac Community
and to Agnes who encouraged me to write:
to Paul for his encouragement and
painstaking editing.

CONTENTS

PROLOGUE

We take time to come aside and rest a little, to rejoice in and enter somewhat the wonder of our being. These are precious days, for we are going on a journey. A journey with the One and with one another. A journey of transformation.

We come as we are, accepting in love that which we are, the selves we know now, and those to be revealed. We care for the soul, the essence; we allow ourselves to simply be, to rest in God. We come to know intimately the patterns of our being. We find them, too, in nature, in scripture, in our dreams, in prayer and meditation.

We know in this time that word comes out of silence, just as day comes out of night. We hold the silence precious for deep listening. The heart listens.

We begin by attuning to ourselves in this present moment, and by allowing an image of this journey to come to us. How do you image the beginning of the journey for you? What is it like? What do you feel? Do you know where you are going, or do you come unknowing into a dark night journey? Are you alone, or is someone with you? What is the landscape of your present life? Are you travelling by night or by day? Are you tired or full of energy? Are you fearful or confident?

Perhaps you may find a passage of scripture, a poem, or part of a story which reflects something of how you are at present, as the journey begins. Or you may like to draw your life now as a season.

Above all, you may simply let doing go, and enter into silent simple Being.

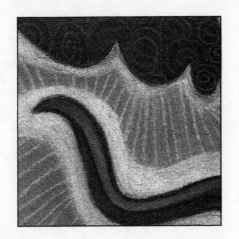

CHAPTER 1

THIS IS MY BODY

Today, we let a question live in us; the question "WHO AM I?" It is a question most central to any journey.

We begin with what is most intrinsically us, our own body. For our own body is a most wondrous universe, a microcosm of the macrocosm, a little universe within the big one. And it houses the Divine. The Divine One, the God, permeates us, every cell of our bodies. We are God-carriers. The meaning of Incarnation is nothing, if not that.

And so we hold our own body, the body of woman, the body of man, in our awareness. Most reverently and gently we hold it.

We experience our way of relating to the body. For this body is miracle, so intricate, with its own language, its own intelligence, its own history, its own experience of pain and delight, its own desire and capacity to heal.

For Indian people, this universe we live in is the Body of God. They know experientially that the same life flows through macrocosm and microcosm. For Body is the form and container of Spirit; each forms and reflects the other; they are inseparable partners.

Spirit, the Breath, the Fire, the Dove, the Wind. The Great Spirit. The One who sometimes blows with the force of a gale, and sometimes breathes as barely perceptible whisper or breath. The Spirit, the One who blows us clean, and who transforms us from within. Attunement to the Breath is intrinsic to our aboriginality, that awareness that body-land and earth-land share one breath, one blood-flow, one heartbeat.

There is a saying in India that any form of meditation must begin with the body, for it is the vehicle of the Self. So, as the poet Kabir suggests, "Stand firm in that which you are"—in your body, in the earth. Feel your body, its language, its pain, its delight. Speak to it and listen to it, for it holds wisdom that is ancient.

Become aware of the flowers or wheels that are located in the different parts of the body. These are the *Chakras*, the centers of all forms of energy. Find them, breathe into them, and let them open out as a flower does. Breathe into the crown of your head, letting the energies of Spirit enter you. Let them flow to the point between your eyebrows, and breathe into the center of vision, faith and insight, the part of us that sees inwardly.

Move to the throat which is the release center for the voice, for speech and song, for the energies of creativity.

Move gently to the center of the chest where the *Heart Chakra* resides, the center of love and compassion.

Breathe four or five breaths slowly, as you focus your attention. Feel your heart. This is the flower at the very center.

Move then to your solar plexus and breathe there. Feel your own personal strength, your capacity to will and decide.

And to the *Sacral Chakra*, the lower abdomen. Breathe there, becoming aware of some of your gut emotions. Breathe into them. Let the flowers open out and clear.

Move then to the *Root Chakra*, becoming aware of your pelvic area. Breathe there, honoring the energies of sexuality and rootedness in the earth.

Sometimes it helps to "feel into" the colors associated with the *Chakras* as the colors of the rainbow.
Red for the *Chakra* at the base of the spine,
Orange for the *Sacral Chakra*,
Yellow for the *Solar Plexus*.
The *Heart* color is *Green*, the *Throat*, *Blue*, the *Third Eye*, *Indigo*, and the *Crown Chakra*, *Violet* or *White* or *Gold*.

Inwardly, see each color as you breathe into its *Chakra*; feel it, too. Can you feel its vibration, its flow? Can you "hear" the color?

We come now to the always amazing words of Jesus, "This is my body." When we say these words to another person, we are giving them our very selves in love, surrender and partnership. They are intimate, naked, vulnerable words we say. This is essence language. We bring to the other the most intimate depth of who we are, and we can give no greater gift. Nor can we receive a greater gift. In the true beauty and mystery of sexual encounter, we also say these words implicitly as self-gift. We stand on sacred ground whenever these are true and mutual words.

In truth, our human body is being groomed, purified and formed for resurrection. And we are partners in the forming. Out of this awareness come profound questions about the relationship each of us has with the outer form of spirit which is ours. Questions of reverence, nurture, life-style, and many others.

There comes a time when the body has done its work. I have encountered a beautiful example of this in a woman who had her feminine organs removed. She attended to her grief. She also negotiated with the medical people to have the organs returned to her, so that she might with full awareness return them to the earth in ritual.

So today, let us become aware of our *"I-am-ness,"* of simply "Being." Let us not need to prove ourselves by doing, and rather than entering our habitual awareness of *"Does-ness,"* let us stand still in the experience of *"I am."*

Let us honor the Body: the great Body of the Universe, the Body of Jesus in Eucharist, and the wonders of our own bodies.

The following suggestions may help you. But they are not meant to be things to "do." Come to them playfully, open, listening. Enjoy them, and give them time.

SUGGESTIONS

1 Read and ponder the words of Jesus: "This is my Body."
2 Draw an outline of your body, and draw or paint the energies—notice the flowing of energies, and where the energies are blocked. What is the flow like? What are the blockages like? Are the energies sharp or soft? What are the colors and textures of the different energies?
3 Dialogue with your body. Use your writing hand for

yourself and let the body respond with the other
hand.

4 Have a meditation in which you anoint your body.
Have soft music, oil, and breathe a mantra or some
other prayer.

5 Ponder Psalm 139.

6 Experience your own *"I-am-ness"* as meditation. If it
helps, say *"I am"* as a mantra, or ponder one of the *"I
am"* sayings of Jesus.

7 Sit on the earth. Be still, feel the earth beneath you.
Listen for its heartbeat.

8 Be still, and open yourself to the spirit of a rock or
tree. Find echoes in the earth from your own spirit.
Let the rock or tree tell you its story.

9 Meditate by opening each of your senses in turn. Look
intently at something for several minutes, then listen
with total attention to a sound. Take your time. Open
the sense of touch by feeling something for several
minutes, then your sense of smell. Finally, spend time
focusing on a particular taste. When all the senses
have been opened individually, experience them all
together.

10 In what ways do you say the words *"This Is My
Body"* in your own life?

11 How do you express your unique *"I-am-ness"* in your
life?

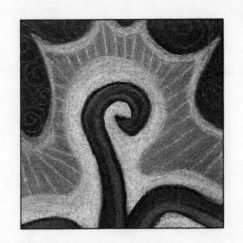

CHAPTER 2

HEARTBEAT

The center of the body is the heart. And one essential thing in this journey to "inward" is to know ourselves as loved and lovable. This applies to God and to other people in our regard, but most of all it applies to us. The hard work we must do is to learn to love ourselves. As Jung said, the task of self-acceptance is one of the most difficult and most necessary of all. For it is to the degree that we love and honor our own being that we are able to truly love someone else or God.

Loving our own being means to love our body, to take care of the soul, to love who we are, to nourish mind and heart. It is most certain that all of us, knowing or unknowing, long most for love. To love and to be loved. Without love we die, or, at the very least, cease to live.

Sometimes we make the mistake that love can be earned. But it cannot be earned, only given. To lover and beloved, this reality is always wonderful and mysterious. It is awesome.

Love is not possessing; often, in fact, it is the pain of letting go. It is not dependency; it is not controlling or being controlled. Nor is it needing or being needed. It is not judgment of the other. It is not the giving and receiving of gifts. Love is eternal. It is of the soul. It is the meeting of two souls in the heart of God. And we are told that God is love.

Some of love's characteristics are trust, forgiveness, compassion, empathy, communion. Perhaps it can best be known by its lack of ego-centeredness. It is not about having and me and mine, but rather about the gift of self to the loved other. It is also about standing in the truth of one's own being, and allowing, indeed affirming and supporting, the otherness of the beloved. It frees rather than constrains. It is honest, and willing to undergo the pain and times of obscurity implicit in loving commitment. It also receives fully the delight, the joy in loving.

Part of the sometimes hard learning we must all do is coming to know experientially that we are, indeed, incredibly loved, just as we are. As John the Evangelist tells us, God first loved us. It seems that sometimes even in a whole life, we may never really experience the utterness of this love that is the root of who we are. The people who have seen it, know it, live it, have a radiance about them.

There were in my childhood pictures of the Sacred Heart, and those pictures spoke a truth. The flower of Jesus' heart was wide open in compassion. The heart of Jesus, the heart of God, the heart of humanity, my own heart. There are many words or phrases to describe how our heart may be at any time—heavy, divided, sick, wounded or broken, burning or sore, warm or kind. In the heart of Jesus we celebrate and participate in a living love, and it is to that living love that the journey takes us. The universe itself may sometimes be experienced as a giant heart beating with love.

We may ponder the particular shape and nature of love energy within us. If, for instance, we draw or paint our own heart, how would we draw or paint it? What would it look like? How was it formed? It is strange that it is quite a simple matter to draw our own heart, and to let it tell its story.

Know that the energies of love are openness and joy and those of non-love are closure and hatred. We may reflect, too, on the family patterns which are imprinted in us and powerfully shape our lives. We may remember patterns of love and of non-love within the family, the love within and between our parents, and the love between siblings. I am reminded of the tragedy of a life depicted in James McAuley's *Because*, in his father's inability to express or receive love. The child's experience of being rebuffed by his father, a momentary event, was lifelong in its effects.

Give yourself lots of time to explore patterns of love and non-love within your family of origin.

How is your heart? Your heart and God? Your heart and others?

The life of the Christian is the gradual transformation of the heart in love. That is the name of the journey of discipleship. And great Christians have known and lived it. Some have prayed the Jesus prayer, or prayer of the heart, as a way of life. Others have spoken of love as a dart of longing from the human heart to the heart of God. The mystics of Christianity, as of other traditions, are people transformed in love. That is the hallmark of the true mystic.

Today, let us enter the mystery of love in our lives. Let us open ourselves to the transforming power of God, to the gift of love in our lives, and to those places where love is absent.

SUGGESTIONS

1 How do you experience love in your life at present?
2 Who are the members of your inner family? How do you relate to each of them? Dialogue with one of the people who lives in you, e.g. your angry self, your sad self, your creative self.
3 Draw as many childhood memories as you can.
4 Imagine you are six years old, and draw a portrait of your family.
5 Remember a time in your life when you knew love. Then remember when love was absent.
6 Remember the happiest experience and the saddest or most painful experience in your childhood.
7 Draw your own heart.
8 Find your own love story in scripture, or tell the story of your life as a love story.

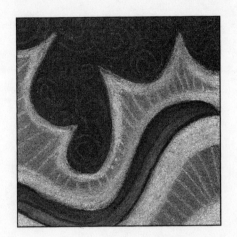

CHAPTER 3

THAT WHICH I AM

In this chapter we will explore a little further the mystery of those words, "I am that which I am." They are the words Jesus spoke to share his essence, his essential self. We, too, may speak these words of our own essential selves. But it is not a matter of speaking them only, but of living into their meaning.

The experience of I-am-ness is an experience of total simplicity and total love. And when we are in our own Being-ness, we are in Being itself.

A child lives in a "being" state very easily, but often in growing up, that capacity for essential simple awareness may be largely lost or overlaid. In a culture which ostensibly devalues the capacity to simply "be," that is certainly so. The journey which we are beginning is a reclaiming of that lost capacity to simply "be." It is so simple, that often we are frightened by it.

This leads us to be aware of a psycho-spiritual insight. It is that the part of us we call "I," the self of which we are aware, is not the center of who we are. The center or essence, the being-ness of who we are, lies much deeper, and the journey home to who we are is a journey to that center.

So, here we are, as a great mystery opens out before us. It is the mystery of our own being, the "terra incognita" of who we are, the revelation of the microcosm within the macrocosm.

The language of depth psychology comes to our aid here. For it acknowledges that "terra incognita" as the unconscious, the not-known of who we are. The pattern of the journey in these terms is the emergence of the conscious self from the deep sea of the unconscious as human life begins, the gradual forming and strengthening of the ego-self which is the primary task of life's first half, and the journey inward as ego becomes aware of and relates to the other side of the self, the unconscious, in the second half of life. Thus, it is a journey to wholeness we are on.

To begin with the self we know, the ego, which holds our conscious sense of "I-am-ness." It is the part of ourselves we identify as "I." It is the "us" through which we experience life, life as it comes from outside us, and life as it comes from within us. It is all that goes to make the "I" that we know. Its life and its capacities are extraordinarily rich. And we must value this "I," for it is most precious.

Interestingly, most forms of ego-centeredness are devaluing of the true "I." Fairly simply, the task we have in relation to the ego is one of befriending, learning actively to like being who we are. Sometimes, as children, we may have received negative and unloving messages about ourselves. If that is so, our task is all the more difficult, but still must be done.

As part of consciousness we also manifest ourselves to the world through the "persona." The word itself means "mask," and describes the different roles we may have, or the image of ourselves we present to the world. There are many "personae," even for one person—teacher, mother, friend, student. Even in the course of one day, we may change the "persona" we wear many times.

The "persona" both reveals who we are to the world, and conceals who we are from the world. It is sometimes a necessary protection for the ego.

It is good to respect our "personae," for often they have taken many years and much labor to build. Sometimes, however, we make the mistake of believing the "persona" is *all* we are. The mother, for instance, may see herself only or primarily as a mother, and so tends to value herself only in that way. It happens then, that when her mothering role is no longer needed, she will experience deep distress. For she has so focused on being a mother that she has never discovered the rich life of her ego-self. She does not know who she really is. When this happens, her life as she has known it breaks down, and in the pain as she opens out to her deeper self, she experiences the breakdown of the self she has known, and the breakthrough of the self she is to become.

The "persona" then, is there for us, not we for it. It is like the clothing we wear: it enhances us, and enables us to be fittingly dressed for certain tasks or occasions. However, it does not determine us. We can change it whenever we wish. Often, in order to grow and to continue the journey, we must leave a particular persona behind, for it is no longer relevant to us. Sometimes, the events of life itself strip us of our "personae." It is as though we are unmasked.

There is no doubt that this journey we are on reveals us to ourselves, and that a deepening self-knowledge is intrinsic to it. It has always been so, for every tradition of inner journey underlines its importance. The necessity of knowing ourselves is a far cry from navel-gazing, for its demands are rigorous and directed to the deepest self. Many centuries ago, the author of the *Cloud of Unknowing* wrote to his readers: "Therefore, strain every nerve and every fiber of yourself to know yourself as you really are. I suspect it will not be long before you know God as God really is."

As life goes on, we do come to a deeper knowledge of ourselves. We learn about ourselves in many different ways: through creative work, through relationships, through understanding the sources of behavioral patterns. We come to recognize the existence of a depth of ourselves which is largely hidden and unknown to us. We are given glimpses of a life below the life we experience, of another language and another way of being. This is the life of the unconscious. It reveals itself to us through dreams and images, through inner connections we perceive, and through experiences that are transcendent.

The unconscious is strange, and at times rather frightening to consciousness, yet, as Jung tells us, it is the medium of our God-experience, and the deepest matrix of who we are. It holds the deep pattern of our being-ness, even the patterns of our ancestry, as far back as it goes. To allow some of these patterns to become part of consciousness, and to recognize the uniqueness of their formation in our own person, is to become a mythmaker. It is an exciting and awesome process, for we find ourselves on sacred ground.

The unconscious, the hidden self, is mysterious, but through the work of explorers of the human psyche we learn that it holds not only the experiences of our personal life, but also certain patterns that are shared by the whole of the human race. As life goes on, and especially in times of life transition, consciousness encounters some of these patterns or energies, and if they are rightly related to, significant growth takes place. A new consciousness is born.

In this process, which is the birth of consciousness to previously hidden aspects of ourselves, we come to recognize the shadow, the hidden and often rejected parts of us. We also come to know our inner masculine and feminine selves, the energies of wisdom and power that are there for us, and the God who is the very center of ourselves.

In this journey, we move toward what could be described as an inner marriage. The opposites in us, the known and the unknown, the strong and the weak, the man and the woman, the soul and God, gradually meet one another. In opening ourselves to this harmony and transcendence, we are doing our life's work.

Inevitably, on the way, we ask the question, though it may not be in the following words, "Who is God for me?" Who or what is this hidden mystery, this inner meaning, this One who is the center, circumference and whole of who we are? It is good for us to live that question at our deepest level.

Perhaps there is an image, a feeling, a sensation or a thought that comes to us. Or we might ask ourselves whether we live our lives out of this inner sense of the One who is infinite. We may find, for instance, that while we say we know a God of love, we, in fact, live our lives filled with fear of many things. If image and life are split, we may need to allow them to come closer to one another.

These insights are the barest hints of ways in which we might open ourselves to the mystery and wonder that lives within us. Once open, the psyche itself, as it were, takes us by the hand and leads us. The experience of revelation is like a birth. A new awareness breaks through to consciousness out of the dark mystery of the unconscious. Like a birth there is pain and struggle, especially just before the birth happens. Like a birth, the newborn awareness is a gift of joy, energy and life. In receiving it, we cannot remain as we were. We are newborn, a little more truly "I am."

SUGGESTIONS

1 Spend some time being still, and simply observe what is happening in you. Draw or describe in writing what happens. Let the active imagination come out of feeling rather than thinking.
2 Complete as many open-ended sentences as you can beginning with "I" or "I am."
3 Notice what place you, the dreaming ego, has in your dreams.
4 Can you feel or see the shape or pattern of your own story?
5 Name some of your "personae." Draw them. How do you relate to each of them? Have a written dialogue with one of them.
6 Remember a time when one of your "personae" left you.
7 Can you remember any dreams to do with clothing or baggage?
8 In what way does the unconscious give glimpses of its life to you?
9 Describe the times in your life when you knew you were standing on sacred ground.
10 What are some of the opposites you experience in yourself?
11 What is the image of God you articulate—the one you live out of?

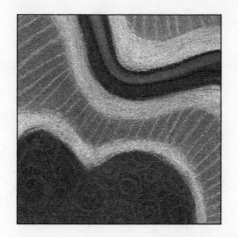

CHAPTER 4

THE FUGITIVES

As life unfolds, parts of ourselves become known to us and others remain hidden. These hidden aspects we know as the shadow.

Ego and shadow are not at ease with one another. Indeed, consciousness frequently experiences the shadow aspects of ourselves as the enemy. Shadow and ego tend to play an ongoing game of hide-and-seek. There is both fear and fascination between them.

But there comes a time when some of our shadow aspects want to move out of darkness at least into partial light. Consciousness, fearful of losing control, resists. But if it is for our wholeness, shadow will persist, and ego must learn to surrender its autonomy, in order that these lesser known parts of us may be recognized, owned and eventually integrated.

What is this shadow? It is an important question, for we cannot overestimate its significance in relation to who we are. It is often seen to be the unloved, inferior or beggar parts of ourselves. The parts of us that we experience as being weak or crippled, the parts we tend to despise and pretend do not exist.

But there is a mystery about the shadow, and it is this: the least-loved part of who we are is not insignificant as we like to think, but is the very key to our potential wholeness. Something of this mystery is expressed in these familiar words, "The stone which the builders rejected has become the cornerstone."

In spite of its tendency to hide from us, shadow does give us glimpses of itself if we are attuned to catch them. Shadow often reveals itself in our dreams. Or it may be that we come to be aware that we are seeing an unrecognized part of ourselves in another person or group of people. Again the shadow may pop out in some form of irrational behavior.

Let us take a dream. A person may dream that they or someone else in their dream is doing violence to another person, even killing them. The dream is showing us precisely and symbolically what is happening within us at the time of the dream. Consciously, we may insist that we would never kill another person. But perhaps if we examine ourselves attentively, there may be someone we would like to be rid of. Or again, it may be that there is a violent part of us which threatens and even destroys a defenseless part of ourselves. We may not be aware of that inner violence.

Sometimes we find we have an irrational reaction to another person. When we are in their presence, it is as though something irrational takes us over. It may be fear, hatred or anger, or, conversely, adulation or wonderment. It is as though a switch is turned on in us. We lose objectivity, and, as Jung would say, are taken over by an affect. We are, in a real way, possessed. We are not ourselves. This phenomenon, known as projection of the shadow, happens when, failing to recognize certain qualities or energies in ourselves, we see them and react to them in someone else.

It is important at these times to locate precisely what it is about the other person which "hooks" this response in us. The irrationality of our response is the indicator that the very thing we either hate or adulate is the very thing that is hidden in shadow in us and to us.

Once we can own this shadow aspect of ourselves, we can withdraw the projection, no longer giving it power over us. We can begin a truthful relationship with the other person as he or she really is. There is always growth in relationships when projections are withdrawn. We are certainly victims of projection when we are blaming everyone or, for example, when we are convinced we are being persecuted; whenever, in fact, we are failing to name or own our personal reality, and transferring it somewhere away from ourselves. Jesus recognized this and described it when he asked, "How can you remove a splinter from someone else's eye when you cannot see the beam in your own?''

The recognition of projection is not a small gift, for we are recognizing latent energies in ourselves. It may be that these energies are destructive of life in us and need to be transformed, or it may be that they are life-giving energies which need to be freed for the enrichment of our lives.

Shadow is revealed, too, at these times when we have an unguarded or unexpected feeling response. An emotion comes out that we didn't know was there. It takes us over at vulnerable times. We feel we are not being ourselves, or that we are out of control.

These manifestations, although the experience can be painful or unpleasant, are actually precious revelations. The shadow being revealed is primitive and clumsy, like a child who is inept. The child needs patience and acceptance, and so does the shadow. It is not evil, but rather rejected, unowned or repressed. When consciousness begins to own it, something good happens, perhaps compassion towards the weaker parts of ourselves, or the recognition of a destructive pattern.

There is a simple principle in this. If we reject or ignore any part of ourselves, that neglected or unaccepted part will revenge itself. Instead of working with us, it will work against us. If, on the other hand, we receive and even befriend our wounded or unloved parts, they will gradually gain the confidence and ability to work with us. They will show themselves to be, as Jung says, ninety percent solid gold.

The shadow is not so much evil; it is rather the unloved, unrecognized, feared and unbefriended part of ourselves. It has destructive power because of our unawareness.

It is true that we cannot be life-giving people in a world that seems in many ways to be in the grip of its own shadow elements (for shadow is hidden in the collective human as in the individual), unless we are consciously addressing our own personal shadow. Unless we are doing this for ourselves, we have no ground to stand on for anyone else. The base for attention and compassion in the macrocosm is in the attention and compassion, the listening heart in the microcosm.

Many fairy tales give us a key to the nature and preciousness of shadow. One such is the well-known story of the princess and the frog. You may remember how the princess was playing with her golden ball one day when she lost it in the pool. She was very distressed, for it was her most precious possession. An ugly old frog hopped up to her and offered to retrieve it, but only on condition that she let him come into her castle and live with her. Of course, she was so anxious to get the ball back that she promised immediately. When she had her ball again, she was so happy that she ran off and completely forgot the ugly old frog. That evening there was a knock at the door (shadow has many ways of knocking on doors). And guess who it was! The royal family were at table, and the princess wanted to forget her promise to the frog. But the king, her father, was there, and he reminded her that she must do what she had promised. So, unwillingly she let him in. Once in, the frog was not happy to be given some food in a corner. He insisted that he share the princess's meal. She was very unhappy, and even moreso when he was determined not only to come to her bedroom with her but to share her bed.

The poor princess! She cried and had a tantrum, but no matter what she did, the frog would not relent. Eventually, worn out, she surrendered. (That word "surrender" is an important one.) And, amazing moment! When she surrendered, the ugly old frog became who it truly was, the most handsome prince. Of course, they married and lived happily ever after.

Often, we too, like the princess at the beginning of the story, remain half people. Perhaps we deny or repress the awareness and valuing of our earthiness, our sexual energy, or our sensual nature.

Shadow, of course, shows itself in our dreams. In a way we cannot generalize about shadow symbolism in dreams. But in dreams, too, shadow is most like what it is: hidden, unknown, strange to us, and sometimes frightening, because it's natural to fear what we do not know.

In my experience, shadow in dreams may be monstrous in some way, or perhaps a person unknown to us or disliked by us. It may be the darkness of night, people who are featureless, or groups of people all alike and foreign to us.

The deep desire of the different parts of us is to befriend us. But sometimes they are not able to befriend us, perhaps because consciousness fears being invaded or overwhelmed, perhaps fears or is unwilling to change certain attitudes, or simply likes control and safety. Yet, if we evade or avoid shadow when the time is right for it to come into the light, we are evading an essential component of the journey to the fullness of who we are. Indeed, we will never come to know who we are.

Shadow is the key, the cornerstone, the hundredth sheep, or the coin that is lost. There is truly great joy when shadow comes into light and we claim it as our own.

SUGGESTIONS

1 Do a spontaneous drawing of your shadow.
2 Dialogue with a shadow figure in your life—maybe another person or a dream symbol.
3 Reflect on dreams you have had in the past in which there has been a manifestation of shadow.
4 Name the times when you have recognized a projection. How did you deal with it? What happened subsequently?
5 Find your own story of shadow and light in a fairy tale.
6 Where are we told of Jesus' encounter with shadow?
7 Draw your shadow
   a) when it is an enemy;
   b) when it becomes a friend.
8 Draw the pattern of the meeting of light and shadow in you.

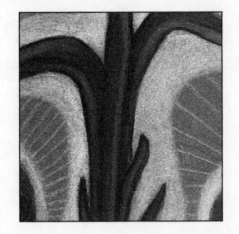

CHAPTER 5

LION AND LAMB

Here we will open our awareness to the opposite and complementary energies of yin and yang. They are the male and female energies which form the partnering in every aspect of life in the universe.

The terms masculine and feminine, as we are using them here, do not apply specifically to men and women, but rather to two opposing and complementary principles of life. The masculine is the active principle and the feminine the receptive principle of life.

To give some indication of the differences in these two forms of energy, I will simply list some words which apply to each. As you read them, see if you can "feel" the energy inside the words.

For instance, what does the word "overpower" feel like? What other words connect to the feeling? How has the word "overpower" been spoken in your own story?

So, let's look at and feel some of the words that hold masculine energy, some nouns, some verbs, some adjectives—active, phallus, pen, knife, sword, gun, arrow, mountain, heaven, fight, march, overpower, master, logos, hierarchical, disparate, penetrate, objective, direct.

The masculine awareness is oriented to power, action and achievement. Its shapes are often straight or sharp. It sees people and things as an hierarchical arrangement, and also sees things in their separateness. Masculine awareness objectifies.

The feminine awareness is opposite in every way. It is an awareness not so much of power and achievement, but of relationship. Its shapes are flowing and its lines curved. It sees people as relating and working together and as intrinsically equal. Rather than seeing things in their separateness, its awareness is global and diffuse, and tends to see things in patterns.

Some words which hold something of feminine energy are womb, cave, cup, water, earth, night, valley, spin, weave, dance, bake, eros, relate, global, diffuse, subjective, permeate, indirect.

Can you hear the difference in these two energies? Which of the words do you "feel" into more easily?

Of course, both male and female energies are in every person, and in each of us there is some form of interplay between them.

We now know the feminine energies in the human person as the "anima" and the masculine energy as the "animus."

I invite you to spend some time in being present and attentive to the movement of these opposite and complementary aspects in your own being, for their activity in relation to one another is happening all the time. Sometimes one is so powerful that it pushes the other out of awareness. When that happens the repressed one builds enormous strength in the unconscious, and will, if not owned and integrated, become destructive. Because they are opposites and so unknown to the other, there is a certain fear and antagonism between them. To allow them to befriend one another within us is the great task confronting us all, and is often what crisis in mid-life is inviting us to. Sometimes the masculine and feminine energies meet within us and flow perfectly in union. That experience, which is really an inner marriage, is a blessed one. For we know, even temporarily, the experience of wholeness.

But most of us are "on the way to the wedding" most of the time. And there are certain ways in which we are able to recognize some aspects of what is happening both in the flowing and in the blocking of these primal energies.

Persons who are strong in animus energy are powerful, outgoing, and achievement oriented. Their pride is frequently in physical prowess and in mastery over situations and people, in having "clout." The awareness is one which tends to order and categorize, and to structure life in hierarchical form. It is a powerful energy of domination. When it flows strongly and well, and is both skilled and compassionate, it has great benefits.

By itself, however, it is one-sided and incomplete. For, if it is by itself, it is "per se" repressing its other side, and unless the two work together the person's awareness and ability to live life fully is severely handicapped. When this happens, and the person is in authority over others, those others tend to become victims.

Indeed, the repressed other cries out for its right to live. When this happens, the masculine energy finds itself being taken over by moods which it can neither account for nor control. Because it is out of touch with its feeling world, those denied or denigrated feelings will gather and rise up, intending destruction to the person. Or it may be that the animus will find himself being ridiculously small-minded and petty, and without a rational base. Or again, he may enter endlessly into dialogue that is pseudo-intellectual and empty of essence. At such times, he is being taken over by the rejected inner woman.

It is then to our own cost if, when the time is right, we refuse entrance to what Jung would call our contrasexual self, whether masculine or feminine.

Feminine or "anima" energy is a receptive flowing energy. Its desire is "eros" or relationship. This energy cannot be circumscribed inside straight lines, for its form parallels the infinite shapes and patterns of nature. It is a mobile energy, diffuse in its awareness, and able to perceive connections that lie beyond a linear time frame or certain set ways of thinking. It is earthed energy. When it flows freely, it is indeed an energy of great beauty and closeness to the essence of life. But, like its counterpart, it is incomplete by itself.

When the inner woman does, however, open herself to her male counterpart, she finds within herself new awareness and new capacities, capacities of strength, initiative and leadership. She allows to unlock, from within her own being, gifts of intellect and clear thought. It does not mean, of course, that such capacities haven't been there, but now there is awareness, precision, vision and other-directedness.

When, however, the "anima" energy neglects or represses her masculine side, he becomes angry, and will take her over in negative ways. She or he becomes the sort of person who is manipulative, who rides roughshod over people, who nags, who expresses ill-thought-out opinions strongly, and will listen to no one.

The energies of "anima" and "animus" in us are, as it were, "ensouled" in us from our parents. It is, therefore, good to reflect on our perception of masculine/feminine relating both within and between our parents. For there we have a mirror of their lived attitudes, some of which also live on in us.

The quality of relationship of the sexes within us is an indicator of our own health and well-being as sexual people. We are encouraged to ask searching questions of ourselves. What are my sexual attitudes and how have they been formed? Do I honor and give space to the sexual energies within me?

Other indicators are there in the way men and women relate in our dreams. Or in the dream interplay of straight lines or sharp edges and flowing mobile shapes and patterns. And how do I relate to men and to women in my life? Confidently? Awkwardly? Avoiding? Freely? Joyfully?

Each day and each moment we continue on the way to the "wedding." A wedding happily consummated in a dream indicates an actual union of these energies within us at a given time in the journey. Out of such union, a child may be born.

Today, let us honor and express the masculine and feminine energies in us in their separateness and in their union.

SUGGESTIONS

1 **Draw or paint the flow and interaction of masculine and feminine energies in you at present.**
2 **Reflect on the gift of an intimate relationship, and on the particular interplay of masculine and feminine energies in it.**
3 **Reflect on some times in your life when these energies were out of balance. What happened?**
4 **Is there one or other energy, masculine or feminine, that you do not acknowledge or honor in your life? What needs to happen?**
5 **Dialogue with your inner masculine or your inner feminine. Draw him or her. What is he or she like? Do they have names?**

6 Undertake some forms of activity or awareness that express a male or female energy source, e.g. for male— a strong physical energy, discipline, some form of active achievement.

For female, experience nurturing the environment through, e.g. aromatherapy or the creation of something beautiful.

Have a time of meditation in which you anoint your body.

Nurture your own life or another's life in some way.

7 Create a total healing environment which expresses both masculine and feminine energies.

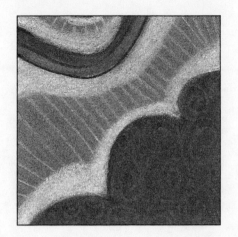

CHAPTER 6

THE GOLDEN CHILD

The child, still drowsy with sleep, holds a candle. Her eyes are filled with dreams. Sweetly shy, a timid smile lights her face. The light seems to come from somewhere inside. She always smiles, rarely laughs. Her laugh, when it comes out from the dark corridors of pre-memory, is the delicate tinkle of tiny silver bells or the cascade of waterfall. But the smile! It is always there. It holds steady through all weathers. The light blossoms in her smile, breaking open as welcome and understanding. But in the very next moment it conceals, and the tiny child is an enigmatic Mona Lisa. Behind it, diffidence crouches, and sometimes agony, or again an inner expansion of excitement or delight.

Her years add up, and as they do, the smile turns into weapon. It becomes engraved as defence. But always it is there.

Her story could be told in the smile, even to the point of contortion. Where is she in that nether moment when agony and ecstasy are held in embrace? And still the smile is there. Will her death mask smile, I wonder?

She probably didn't know what to do with the pain. So she smiled, and everyone thought "what a happy child!" She wasn't unhappy either. For she did have a secret world inside herself which was mysterious and had quite a lot of beauty. She liked being there, playing her happy games without fear.

All the same, fear lurked. Like a sleek gray wolf, it hovered outside the gate of who she was. And sometimes she could see a dark shadow, not just one but many, which seemed to slink around and even pierce the walls. Then she would hide so as not to be seen. She learned quickly to keep away and not be a nuisance. Fear came when she was scorched—by burning wind, relentless summer sun, or anger. Then she shrivelled and her delicate freshness, at least on the outside, became dry and withered. The anger scorched her skin which was defenseless. Especially her face. Only much later did she discover the anguish buried in her face.

The child's body was fine-tuned, too much so. The word "trauma" comes, but in what context or how, is only dimly guessed. Some cruelty, some shock, perhaps abandonment. Yes, perhaps abandonment, the too-sudden change from encircling arms and gentle sounds to the cold hard contours of hospital bed and impersonal voices. Yet, she survived—no, not survived, lived.

There was always a pattern of emergent life from threatened death. Hard to imagine its form, except to know that life hid itself somewhere in the profoundest cavity of death's shape. How could anyone know it was even there? A tiny invisible spark. Death must eventually crumble in the face of its naked fire. Yet the fingerprints of death remained.

And so the child. She stands there with her candle, timid, exploring, tentative on the edges of joy. She waits. There is trepidation in her waiting. And anticipation. A sort of suspended excitement. Almost wonder. The fear came back in different ways—in the giant destructiveness of a tidal wave, though even in the moment of greatest fear she could still be overawed by its beauty. It could annihilate, but didn't. Or was it a giant hand that descended in the night and threatened to smother, but couldn't? The spark was too strong.

There is a memory imprint there. She was about two years old. Her mother held her hand while a doctor examined her baby sister. Why that memory? Why not something else? Only now she knows that at that moment she was happy. Her mother was holding her hand. In that moment she was there for her, just for her. There is, even now, a sense of pride and well-being in that moment. Perhaps it was rare that it happened just that way.

Her stomach was always a trouble. She was born without acid in her system. Struggling to digest, she was unknowingly malnourished. A carsick child. Fragile. Tough too. Body bore and reflected her most intimate experiences with terrifying accuracy. But Body was a friend. It fought against the self-destruct of unawareness. It wanted to live, to let its rigid lines relax into the beauty of curve, and its fear-filled cells to know love. Body worked in the night.

Her mother said she was a little wanderer. She loved to wander. An explorer. A creature of solitude. Away from this earth, and on this earth. Breaking new ground. Always the next step, with destination to be revealed. But go on she must.

This is the story, or part story, of a child. The child who is parent of the adult. It grew from the contemplation of a childhood photo.

Of all the weaving threads and patterns that combine in the tapestry of our personal story, none is more crucial, more powerful or more able to hold our essence than is the inner child.

Just as scripture describes the "contraries," the lion and the lamb lying together in harmony and led by the child, so does it happen in the human psyche. The child reconciles the irreconcilable, heals the wound, lives in the radiance of the divine.

Perhaps at times we glimpse the child within in moments of spontaneity, transparency, playfulness, shyness, friendliness, fear or defiance.

What is the child within us like? Do we know her? Can we visualize him? Do we spend time with her? Sometimes we may experience this child as the one who tyrannizes us. Perhaps he is sick or hurting, maybe even dead.

It is strange that the wound we received in our earliest most vulnerable state is the cradle of selfhood. Indeed, it seems that in one way or another, most of us experienced abandonment in one of its many forms. This was the wound.

It was a totally devastating experience, but how amazing! We didn't die. For in this wound, as a flower is buried in the deepest part of a bud, was formed the shape and pattern of our uniqueness. In it, the soul was forged. In it, the creative potential of our lives was hidden.

The child who lives in the deepest center of who we are is the matrix of that creative potential. In each release of true creativity, this child is born again.

The child was born once, and is continually born again. The pattern of the birthing is repeated, perhaps at another level and in other aspects of emergent personhood, but in essence the pattern is likely to be that of the initial birth. While the experience of our birth is a pre-memory event for most of us, the body and the psyche carry not only the memory but the lived experience of birth, and they do not lie to us.

What is the story of your birth? Have you heard something of it from others? Your mother, perhaps? More importantly, how have your life patterns revealed to you something of your birth-pattern? Were you a baby who resisted leaving the security of the womb and now clings to those things that give security? Or was your coming into the world enthusiastic and confident? Whatever the particular pattern of your continuing birth, recognize it, welcome it, and learn from it.

Perhaps, too, your childhood struggles played (and play) themselves out in some part of your body—a nervousness, a heaviness, a fiery energy, a sensation of sharpness and tingling. The body knows our story best. It remembers everything, and carries in its cells the inside story of every event. The body is always telling us our story if only we can listen.

Perhaps the child comes into our dreams—ourselves as a child or groups of children. Are the children who come into our dreams happy, or sick, or distressed, or mischievous?

In our own story, which of our child energies were freed and valued and encouraged? Which of them did we have to hide or build some form of pretense or defense around? What were the protective walls we built for our survival? Perhaps they are still there, even though we are adults now and have no need of them any more.

It is significant, too, that the ground of grace in our Western culture is a tiny child. The baby of Bethlehem is the Golden Child. One side of our culture so powerful and achieving, and in the shadow of its power a helpless baby. Paradoxically, it is not the power that exploits but the baby, the Golden Child, who holds the key to all that is true and lasting and beautiful in our way of life.

Today, let us celebrate the child within us and spend time with him or her. For just as we need the child to live fully into our lives, so does the child need us.

SUGGESTIONS

1 Dialogue in writing with your child. Use your writing hand for your part in the dialogue and your nonwriting hand for the child's.

2 Imagine yourself, as you are now, going back to your childhood home (or somewhere else) and meeting your child. What happens?

3 Finish these open-ended sentences for each stage of your life:

When I was five...

When I was seven...

When I was ten...

etc.

4 Take your child and do something you both enjoy.

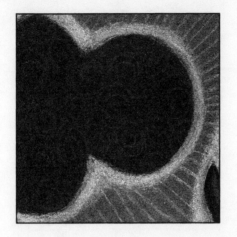

CHAPTER 7

THE SEER SEES

We see with our two eyes. We marvel, not only that we can see, but also at what we see, the infinite variations of color, shape and pattern that are there for us to look at every day. Often though, we are so busy, or so caught up in our concerns, that we do not see. Our eyes are blind to the wonders around us.

We may ask ourselves what is the particular character of our seeing. What do we notice—colors, shapes, fine detail or flowing patterns?

As well as our outer seeing, there is a way of seeing inwardly. We have a third eye or inner eye. It is the eye through which we perceive inner reality, and more abstract things like goodness or truth, wisdom or love. And just as the outer eyes are bathed in revelation if they are open, so is the inner eye.

We will ponder and experience the capacity to see inwardly, especially through the revelatory language of the symbol, the dream and the myth.

The language of symbol mediates between the conscious and the unconscious, between the outer eye and the inner. That is why it can express what is inexpressible in any other way. It is the language which comes to us when we try to share an experience that seems to have no words, because it is different from our ordinary experience. An experience of God is like that.

The symbol is itself, and also points to something beyond itself. It holds meaning and energy for us that points to the infinite. We can never exhaust the meanings that a true symbol holds for us. The symbol can hold the opposites, too, just as the sea holds both terror and beauty, or the rose has both scent and thorns.

How does a symbol happen? It seems that there are certain patterns or archetypes imprinted, as it were, in each of us. They are the patterns of our human story. When we meet one of these patterns in nature, or in a happening, there is immediate recognition or resonance. There is a shared pattern, a shared energy. That happening or that pattern in nature becomes a symbol for us and evokes a deep, intuitive feeling response.

Let me give a simple example. A young woman who had lived all her life in the cane-field country in northern Queensland would not miss the burning of the cane fires at night. She would come a great distance to see the burning cane. It was a symbol for her. Two things spoke to her in the cane-fire symbol. One was the beauty of the flames in the night; the other was the burning away of what was inessential to the pure sugar. In that simple experiential awareness of the symbol, the young woman knew her own self and the shape of her story.

It is good to walk among our symbols. We all have many, though we may not acknowledge it. But we do live a symbolic life. And through that life, the Divine is revealed to us.

When images and symbols are woven together they may form a song, a poem, a fairy tale or myth, a story that lives on in us, a dream, a dance, or a work of art. Our own story is woven in this tapestry of symbol.

The threads and colors of the tapestry are shown to us in our dreams. In the language of symbol, our dreams reveal to us our own truth. They open to us the innermost aspects of who we are. They tell us the ongoing story of our own being. They heal us, enlighten us and challenge us.

Often the dream will give us a message about something we need to know, but which our conscious mind cannot apprehend. The dream seeks to balance, to give the other side of our conscious awareness. The unconscious has a different and deeper knowing than consciousness, and, for the full living of life, we need both. The dream, whether it is a dream in sleep or a waking dream, as a vision or meditation, gives us this deep knowing.

The dream is actually an inner symbolic picture of us as we

truly are at the time of the dream. And so each of its component symbols are aspects of us.

It is good to wonder about our dreams, to come to them with great reverence and a listening heart. To ask, too, what they are telling us about ourselves, and the inner attitudes in our lives at the time of the dream. Or to sit in the dream, to let ourselves imaginatively become one of its symbols, to question, and to listen. For the dream is always trying to heal, to balance, to help us to see what is really happening.

What are the feelings in your dreams, the complexities, the conflicts, the wounds, or, conversely, the joy and the full flow of life? What questions would you like to ask of the dream? What is it telling you about your life, your inner attitudes?

Perhaps you have a dream that keeps coming back in one form or another. It seems to be trying to tell you something you haven't yet been able to hear. When you do hear, it will not need to come back any more.

In some tribal groups, the leader was known to be the one who was given dreams to guide the whole community. And the one who listens to the dream and speaks its revelation in life is wise.

Carl Jung described a process of journeying which he called "individuation." It is the capacity of the person to live fully into his or her unique reality, to live one's own pattern of personal wholeness. The dream reveals to us the day-by-day pattern of that journey.

Another way in which the story is revealed is through the myth. A myth is a sacred story, a story of truth or meaning told in the language of symbol. It is the story of our essential or eternal being. When we are ready and sufficiently attuned to receive revelation from the unconscious, it tells itself to us. Or, more truly, it lives itself in us.

To open our hearts to the sacred story we live, we enter an awareness of the meaning of our life. What does our life want? What does it seek? What are its patterns?

And what are the symbolic patterns that hold the story? Patterns of journey, of dawn breaking out of a dark night, of finding the beauty in something thought to be ugly, of ice becoming flowing water?

What is your story?

The myth is lived in timeless time. It is our eternal story, the never-ending story. We are all makers of myth. And the myth reveals to us who we are, who we are as an individual, and who we are as a people.

Sit very still, and let your sacred story tell itself to you. Let it come from the unconscious, and be reverently received by consciousness. I promise you will not be bored for one moment.

So today, let us wander among our symbols, listen to our dreams, and live into the sacred story of who we are.

SUGGESTIONS

1 Sit in a time of quiet meditation, and write the stepping stones (ten or twelve events) of your story. Begin "I was born... and then... and then." Don't try to "think" the stepping stones. Take time and let them come spontaneously. Jot down a word, a phrase, a sentence for each. Meditate on what your stepping stones reveal to you. What patterns do they reflect back to you?

2 Describe a symbol. Why is it symbolic for you?

3 Write a significant dream, and spend time befriending it. What does it reveal to you? Live into the dream. Share it with someone.

4 Prepare to enter your own myth through the following steps:

a) Write a short statement of the meaning of your life as you understand it. "The meaning of my life is..." Meditate on what you have written.

b) Meditate on your stepping stones. Write feeling words or accompanying memories around each.

c) Walk among your symbols. Let them reveal the symbolic pattern of your story to you.

d) Let memories come to you, from childhood, adolescence, the different periods of adulthood. Write them down.

You may do any or all of these things in a playful and childlike manner. Your story will begin to tell

itself to you when it is ready. You may like to begin
"Once upon a time..." or "Many years ago..."

Or you may like to write your story as an
historical account or a poem, or in some other way.
Be creative.

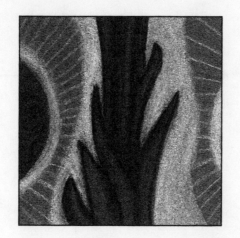

CHAPTER 8

SEASONS

We enter the mystery of time in our lives—the past, the present, the future, and the timeless time in which our mythology is woven. Some people call it eternity, where "all is always now."

Time *is* a mystery, especially the time before and during and after the time that moves in a straight line. This is the timeless time which holds the patterns of our ancestry, the seasons of the human journey, and the seasons of our own particular journey.

Time is seasonal. Our lives are an ever-deepening living into the springs, the summers, the autumns and the winters. We live into the patterns of the newly-born in springtime, of fruitfulness in summer, of gentle dying in autumn, and of death and nakedness in winter.

Our springtimes come when something new is born into our lives. A new love, a new energy or inspiration, a new expression of the creative spirit that lives in all of us.

When we reflect on life's springtimes we may become aware of the ways in which life's newness presses in, or bursts in, or creeps in on us. The birth of anything new is both wonderful and frightening, for the unknown hides there. As well as the newness of experience, we meet the strange and little-known parts of ourselves. The person we were is no longer there, and we do not yet know the new us. But everything is touched with the fresh beauty of leaves and buds opening out in spring. Wonder, joy and delight are the words of this season. Perhaps as we reflect, our felt memory brings to us the times in our lives that have been springtimes.

In the summer we know ourselves as mature, and producing fruit for the sustenance and delight of our human family. It is the time of life's fullness and its fruitfulness. It is the time of plenty, the time when we feel and know what Jesus meant when he said that our fullness of life was the reason for his coming.

Sometimes we meet people who radiate a sense of life's fullness to us. They are the people who are filled with true joy, who are self-aware but not self-centered, and who bring a full and compassionate heart to their way of being with others.

Autumn is perhaps the most beautiful of all the seasons, a season of color, of mist, of gentle sunshine and changing moods. It is probably meant to be the most beautiful of seasons in life's journey too. It is our time of aging and dying, often as nature does, graciously and gracefully. There is a sadness about autumn too, for it is a time of loss and of letting go. A time of surrender.

In our lives, the autumns are those times of slow dying. Perhaps it is a time of the death of a relationship, or the slow finishing of a creative task in which we have given fully of ourselves. There is often a greater gentleness in us, a mellowing of attitudes, a serenity. It is the season of contemplation.

And winter. The season of death, of nakedness, of life's hiding. Birds and animals hide away. They, as it were, go underground. In their own ways, humans hibernate too. Life withdraws and disappears. We wait in the long cold winter for spring to come.

The winters of our lives are like this also. There is some form of death, of stripping, and we cannot perceive or feel life's warmth and movement. It is as though we are in some way frozen up. Perhaps it is a parting that numbs us, or the dying of someone dear to us. Perhaps a loss of something, a home, or a situation that has nourished us. We are only able to stay there and endure this winter. But as we endure, the thin web of our faith tells us that sometime, somehow, spring will come again.

Our human lives are cyclical and ever-deepening. We live through their seasons, each one enriching us in wisdom, each one revealing a pattern in our story.

I love to think of life, too, as the weaving of a great tapestry, rich in color and motif, some of the themes bold and strong, others delicate and subtle. Or as a song that is sung, or a dance that is danced.

The seasons are lived in the lives of men and women, and the Christ seasons in the lives of Christians. Even the dying and rising of Jesus is a story of seasons. Holy Thursday is a day of sharing, joy and heartbreak. Good Friday is a winter day or season, a time of death, confusion, pain and stripping. Holy Saturday is a season of burial, of hiddenness, of unknowing. And Easter Sunday, the time of radiance, of delight, of restored hope. The seasons of human life are lived in those days of dying and rising.

And so, the mystery of time in our lives. And the praying memory that reclaims time's wastelands by learning to love them.

We do have a sense of time in our lives that has nothing to do with chronological time, nor with chronological age. So at any moment in the journey, it may be morning, the time of awakening and new hope, or midday, the time of active involvement. Or perhaps it is evening, when we learn to rest and be gentle. Or the darkest of dark nights, when we cannot see and do not know. When we seem to be submerged in darkness.

So today, let us enter the mystery of time in our lives. Let time enfold us and befriend us. Let the seasons of our lives speak their words to us.

SUGGESTIONS

1 **Reflect on your life journey as seasons. When were the times of spring, of summer, of autumn, of winter? Which season are you in at present? Remember and feel some of the events surrounding each of your seasons.**

2 **As a reflection on the seasons of the paschal mystery, take four days of Holy Week: Holy Thursday, Good Friday, Holy Saturday and Easter Sunday. Write as many words or phrases as you can for each one, then question your own heart. Feel into each of these "great" days.**

   Holy Thursday... How am I sharing my heart now?
   Good Friday... What am I suffering now?
   Holy Saturday... What must I leave be for now?

Easter Sunday... What is being born in me now?
3 Read and reflect on Ecclesiastes 3:1–8.
4 Draw a clock-face. What time is it for you? Why do
   you say it is that time?
   Finish the following open-ended sentences:
   It is too soon to...
   It is too late to...
   It is just the right time for...
5 Paint the seasons of your life.

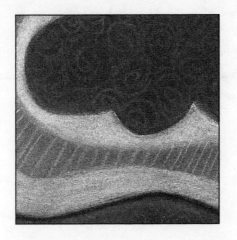

CHAPTER 9

MANDALA

We strive to be whole and well, to live to the fullness of our capacity. This is a desire and an energy that lies deep within us.

There are many patterns of wholeness; sometimes the wholeness of simplicity and unity, and at others the wholeness of parts flowing in harmony. There is the wholeness of sun or moon or newborn baby, and there is the wholeness of day and night, of the four seasons of the year, or of the old man or woman who is ready to die and has come to peace.

This wholeness in our personal lives is born out of the coming together of the opposites within us: joy and pain, doubt and faith, fear and love, birth and dying. The meeting of opposites in the ground of who we are is the work of a lifetime. It is like a gradual birth into essence. In the book of Isaiah there is a wonderful image of this union of person in God-ground in the vision of the lion and the lamb lying down together, and the child leading them. In another talk we have entered somewhat into the mystery of the child, and his or her centrality in the heart of who we are. It is the child within us who can best unite and lead our warring selves to peace. A life separated from the child within is existence rather than life.

The seat or ground of our wholeness is what Carl Jung described as the archetype of the Self, or the God-pattern within every person. Different people may use different language to attempt to describe this reality. It is in some way to apprehend or be apprehended by the One, the Breath within the breath, or the

Divine Lover. Each person's pattern of this encounter, which is transforming of life, is unique.

A great and universal image of wholeness is the *Mandala*. The original meaning of the word "mandala" is "circle." A circle is infinite in its form, having no beginning and no end. It also contains and protects what it circumscribes.

Nature is filled with mandalic patterns—the cross section of a branch, the human eye or the human face, the tree with its branches reaching up into the heavens and its roots penetrating deep into earth, or flowers like the lotus, the rose or the daisy. The human body is a mandala with its center, the heart.

There is another word for "making whole." It is the old English word "healing." When a person is, as it were, bathed in the Self, perhaps through an experience of a waking dream or meditation or a profound life experience, healing is implicit. Often, too, the nature of the healing or whole-ing grows out of the nature of the dis-ease.

Jesus, the Divine Healer, understood and practised the inner principles of healing. One of these is that true healing restores the whole person. For sickness or wounding is not only of the body, the mind, the psyche, or the spirit, but of the whole person. Dis-ease may be seen as a blockage in the healthy flow of energy, or wounding as a sharp invasion of the energy field. In some forms of dis-ease, the level of energy flow is very low; in others, the different energies are fighting against one another. Or again, an alien energy may become rampant and take over.

In this matter of healing, the symptom or outer sign of the dis-ease is highly significant. For it is the symptom which reveals truthfully the nature of what needs to be healed. The symptom does not only work on a physical base, but is the physical expression of the inner form of the sickness.

Let me give an example. We speak of the heart in many ways as I have said before—as broken, as burning, as hard, as strong, as pierced. The experience, for instance, of betrayal, could cause a broken heart. Spiritually, the experience could be one of living into the experience of Jesus' betrayal by Judas. Psychologically, it may be consciously to allow ourselves to feel the pain of betrayal, and gradually to befriend that pain. Indeed, there is nothing more heartbreaking, nothing more painful, than to be betrayed by someone we have loved. That pain, strong and sharp as though it is breaking the heart in two, will also be felt in the body.

Each of us is one person. Each of us needs to be aware of the revelation hidden inside the symptom. For most often, the symptom both enfolds and expresses an attitude that needs to be changed and healed, or to be accepted and integrated. Within every person, there is the one who is sick or wounded and also the One who heals. The ministry of Jesus as told in the gospels needs to continue daily in each of us. The wounded need to come to the healer, and the healer to heal. We learn to be compassionate toward ourselves.

There is another element here, and that is the necessity of faith, of that leap beyond the rational, of simply believing that we can be healed. This, perhaps, can be hardest of all. Because believing is rather like being a trapeze artist who has just swung out from the safety of the nets and poles. There is nothing there except a simple steady standing in faith.

It seems strange that sometimes when people are taken a little deeper, they find they do not really want to get well, because it would mean they must change. Their sickness has become a means of defense from life. The challenge of living fully is too great. They choose to continue to be sick.

In another instance, when the time comes and the body has done its work in its own time and way, it ceases to be effective. This process is to be honored and surrendered to. To be fully conscious in it is a great gift.

As we delve into the mystery and wonder of who we are (in ancient days "delving" was a science and art), we may find that the mandalas of our lives with their eternal patterns reveal themselves to us. In that revelation we are shown our soul-colors, the unique patterning of light and shadow, the pattern of wounding and healing, and the shape of our journey to wholeness.

SUGGESTIONS

1 **Reflect on the mystery of wounding and healing in your own life.**

How do your symptoms reflect your inner story?

3 Draw or make a mandala which reflects the nature and flow of your story.

4 What sort of energy heals you? When do you experience this healing energy?

5 How do you see yourself as a wounded healer?

6 How do you give time each day for the energies of healing to flow in you?

7 There is a mantra in the Book of Jeremiah, "You have healed me, and I am healed." Meditate this mantra with your breath.

CHAPTER 10

WHEELS AND FLOWERS

We are learning more now about the fields of energy with which we are surrounded and of which we are part. We know, for instance, that everything has its own energy field or subtle body which protects and nourishes it and interacts with other energy fields. Thus life may be seen as a motion and flow. Sometimes if we look in a certain way by relaxing our eyes, we are able to perceive these fields of energy around a tree, for instance, or, in a certain light, around a person's head. The ability to see in this way can be developed.

So it is that just as there is a macrocosm and a microcosm, universe and person, so there is a universal energy field and a human energy field. These two are constantly in interaction with one another.

Try to imagine the layers of subtle body that surround and penetrate your physical body. To imagine, too, the constant movement of energy both within and around your own body. Sometimes the movement of these energies can be seen as colors. Can you see the movement of energy as well as feel it?

The energy gathers and intensifies in seven centers in the human body. These centers are called *Chakras*, a word which means *a wheel* or *a flower*. The very center of the *Chakras* is the heart *Chakra* which is located in the region of the heart. The heart *Chakra* is the center of love energy, of passion and compassion. The Christian mystical tradition conceives of the human journey as being a gradual transformation in love, a transformation of the heart. Often then, in the practice of contemplative prayer, the loving awareness of God is directed to the heart *Chakra*. If we think of its pattern as a wheel, we are drawn to the hub or the still center; if we think of it as a flower, we feel the heart opening out in compassion. The ancient and loved prayer of the heart unites this heart-attention with the breath and the Name of Jesus.

The points of the *Chakras* in ascending order are the *Root Chakra* which is situated at the base of the spine, the *Sacral Chakra* in the belly, the *Solar Plexus Chakra* seated just below the ribs and meeting the belly button, the *Heart Chakra* in the chest, the *Throat Chakra* in the throat, the *Third Eye* between the eyebrows, and the *Crown Chakra* on the top of the head.

Energy flows in and between the *Chakras*, and each one has its own particular energy form. Indian people like to think of a great serpent coiled at the base of the spine. Gradually it rises and ascends through each of the *Chakras* cleansing it and filling it with energy. The *Chakras* which open out on the front and the back of the body may be imaged as colored vortices spinning in a clockwise direction.

If our *Chakras* are open, we experience ourselves as filled with energy to live fully and creatively. If they are closed, the experience is to feel physical, attitudinal and spiritual blockage.

It is good to take our inner vision to the areas of the *Chakras*, and, if we can, to perceive in these areas both the feeling of color and the nature of movement. We become better at doing this simply by practice. There have also been traditional under-standings of both the colors and the energy patterns in each of the *Chakras*. But anything you read or hear in this matter must be looked at in the light of your own experience.

The energy of the *Root Chakra* plants us firmly in the earth and in our physicality and sexuality. The person who is strong in *Root Chakra* energy is totally present in the moment in an earthy way. The energy color of this *Chakra* is *Red*.

The *Sacral Chakra* holds our gut energy, our gut emotions, and the flow of sexual energy. Sometimes this *Chakra* may be blocked by long-held emotions of anger, grief or fear. Its energy color is *Orange*.

The *Solar Plexus Chakra* mediates the energy of our sense of firm belonging in the universe, of stability in who we are, a positive sense of I-am-ness, and the capacity to take initiatives and to decide wisely. It is the energy of self-confidence and purposefulness. Its energy color is *Yellow*.

Now we come to the central *Chakra*, the *Heart*, the center and channel of our loving. Although its traditional energy color is *Green*, those who have spiritual vision see beautiful configurations of many colors. The person whose primary focus is heart energy will find that with time and consistent focus, the heart energy will first awaken, and then spread to and permeate the other *Chakras*.

The *Throat Chakra* is the *Chakra* of communication, self-expression and creativity. When we are blocked in any of these areas, that blockage will tend to gather in the throat so that we find we cannot hear, cannot swallow (not only physically but in every way), that we have no voice, or that we have not found our voice (that is, discovered the truth of who we are). The energy color of this *Chakra* is *Blue*.

Now we move to the area between the eyebrows where the *Third Eye* is located. It is the eye of intuition, intelligence, vision and faith. It is the eye of which Blake wrote when he said, "If the eye of our perception were cleansed, we would see everything as it is, infinite." Often the human journey may be seen as a gradual opening of the third eye. Such opening out of inner vision was the gift implicit in Jesus' healings of the blind. The energy color of the third eye is *Indigo*.

Finally we come to the *Crown Chakra*. It is seated at the top of the head, and is the entry point of the Spirit. In the profoundest of our experiences of God, this *Chakra* (and possibly the other six) are opened. Likewise in experiences of ecstasy of any kind, sexual, aesthetic, emotional or spiritual, all the *Chakras* may be opened. The energy colors of this *Chakra* may be *Violet*, *White* or *Gold*.

It is a good practice to begin each day by opening the *Chakras*. Notice what each one feels like, and take five deep breaths as you breathe its true color into each of the *Chakras*. Gradually, you will feel movement in these centers of energy. Before and after, it is good to take five deep breaths into the sense of the golden flowing light of the whole person. That is to glimpse the experience of transfiguration or resurrection.

The *Chakras* function on every level of who we are, physically, psychologically, spiritually. If the *Sacral Chakra* is open, front and back, the person has an open healthy relationship to his or her sexual energy, and an appreciation of the delights of sharing sexually. If closed, sexual drive is low and the person tends to devalue the significance and pleasure of sexual sharing. In an experience of sexual sharing that is ecstatic, all the *Chakras* would be open.

As Barbara Anne Brennan, to whom I am indebted for some of the material in this chapter, writes in *Hands of Light*, "The mutual letting go into deep communing through giving and receiving in sexual intercourse is one of the main ways humanity has of deeply letting go of the ego 'separateness' and experiencing unity. When done with love and respect for the uniqueness of your mate, it is a holy experience culminating from the deep primordial evolutionary urges of mating on the physical level, and the deep spiritual yearnings of uniting with Divinity. It is a wedding of both the spiritual and physical aspects of the two human beings." (Bantam, 1987, p.73)

Those whose *Solar Plexus Chakra* is open have a clear sense of belonging and a grounded sense of themselves. They are confident in the taking of decisions, and have an at-home-ness with themselves. When the solar plexus center is blocked, the personal experience is of disconnection, separateness and repressed feelings.

The person with an open *Heart Chakra* is a loving person. Strong heart energies move from her or his heart to the hearts of others. As well as particularity, there is universality about this love. The person is compassionate. The energies of healing pass through this *Chakra*.

The *Heart Chakra* is at the very center of the *Chakras*, and when it is the focus of meditation, love gradually becomes the deep energy which pervades every aspect of life. Rudolf Steiner describes the exquisitely beautiful colors and patterns of the *Heart Chakra*, and many spiritual patterns are based around its opening.

When the *Throat Chakra* is open, we know how to receive what is given us for nourishment at every level, and to sing or speak our particular word or song. Our creative energies are freely and fully expressed. We find our own voice, and lean to speak our truth.

With the open *Third Eye Chakra* we can see clearly, intuit correctly, and know directly. It is the eye of intelligence and vision. If, on the other hand, it is blocked, we will be blind and unaware in some ways. Our thoughts and insights will have a muddy confused quality.

The *Crown Chakra* opens us to the experience of God. If it is closed, the person may know words about God, but is closed off to actual experience of God. When this *Chakra* is open, the person enters into Being, often a blissful experience.

The *Chakras* gradually open through the practice of meditation, and through a full-hearted response to life. One of the simplest and most powerful ways to tend this blossoming is to breathe gently into the whole person, and then into each of the *Chakras*. Breathe in with a sense of motion and color, and above all of the Spirit Who permeates the whole universe, the great universe and the small universe which each of us is.

SUGGESTIONS

1 Draw an outline of your body, and then fill in your energies. Notice where the energies flow, and where they are blocked. Notice their colors and textures, and what they would look like if they need to change.

2 Do a *Chakra* meditation. Take five deep breaths for the whole, then begin at the *Crown Chakra*, taking five deep breaths as you focus your attention there. Feel a sense of color or motion if it helps you. Do this for each of the *Chakras*, then complete the meditation with five deep breaths for the whole person. Play soft music if it helps you.

3 Do a body scan. Imagine yourself travelling through every part of your body. Notice where there is pain or dis-ease and imagine your self working with it to ease or heal. Visualize the healing process happening.

4 Sit very still and blend with what is around you.

5 Look at a scene till it begins to flow for you, and then draw it.

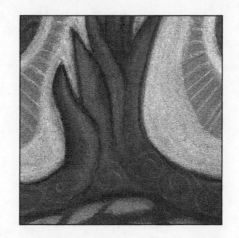

CHAPTER 11

ONLY SITTING

The *Zen* verse which inspired the title of this book goes like
this:
"Sitting, only sitting
spring comes
and the grass grows
by itself."

I want to explore the inner journey as it is expressed in the
practice of meditation or contemplative prayer.

To enter a meditative state is to become at once simple and
focused. When we watch a child or any person doing something
or looking at something with total absorption, that person is
meditating. It is so simple, and often we ourselves may
spontaneously enter certain moments of quiet and total
attention. But for some reason, when we try to do it, it seems to
become difficult.

It is a matter of learning to be still, unless the meditative form
is one of, for example, dance or some art form. But even then, at
certain moments, the movement itself seems to take on a stillness.
One of the psalms holds the two great movements of the
meditative process: "Be still and know. . ." This sounds easy, but
is not. For eventually, the stillness must pervade every fiber of us
and the knowledge is an enlightenment that is given not
attained, and breaks beyond rational knowing.

The way we come to stillness needs to be the way that best suits
us. Posture is important; for example, a straight back. We may
sit, or lie, or stand, or walk. Sitting, particularly, is a centering

posture. Especially if we sit in a cross-legged or lotus posture, the body seems to become a living mandala. And many forms of meditation encourage us to attend to the breath, to attend to what we are doing all the time; that is, breathing. Therefore, when we sit and breathe and are present to ourselves, we meditate.

One of the best ways I have found to describe what meditation is, is the word "blending." A person I know describes how, when she was a child, she would sit perfectly still for hours. Gradually small animals would come to her, and even before they came she would know how they were. She learned to hear the sound beneath the sound, and her senses became so attuned she would pick up the least change, in herself and in the plants and animals around her.

For some modes of life, the practice of meditation is primary, and we may wonder why it is given such prominence, for it seems to achieve nothing.

What it does achieve, in fact, is an inner transformation, first in the little universe which is the human being, and then in the great universe. Carl Jung described this inner transformation as a process, a process of active meditation, or, as he called it, active imagination, through which the individual might gradually discover his or her unique truth or wholeness.

Twice, I had the great privilege of spending time at "Shantivanam," the ashram in the south of India where Dom Bede Griffith lived. I remember arriving there for the first time very early one morning, and feeling in the russet-colored cottages and the luxuriant and brilliantly-colored flowers that here was a place of great joy. My first impressions were not mistaken but confirmed in my first meeting with Dom Bede and in the general happiness that pervaded the whole place. There were many joys, not the least being to hear the reflections of someone with great spiritual insight each day, and to have opportunity to speak with him about my own struggles in the practice of prayer.

I have rarely encountered such quality listening, and he would describe his own practice of meditation as the simple rhythm of breath and mantra. That is the way for many people and an honored path in the Christian tradition, especially in the prayer of the heart or the Jesus prayer. There, one simply looks into one's own heart, while breathing a sentence or phrase with the

Name of Jesus in it. John Main, one of the great promulgators of this way of prayer in the West, suggests *"Maranatha—Come, Lord Jesus"* as the mantra.

The transformation which happens through the meditative process comes from deep within us, from what Jung would describe as the archetype of the Self, or the pattern of Divinity within us. There is no more direct way for this transformation to happen than the opening of our awareness to the presence of God within. And for each person, the pattern of transformation is unique.

That is why there are many different modes of meditation. For many people, a simple mode of centering prayer is the way. A mantra leads them to stillness and silence. They sit still in Being. Often, too, our breathing takes us to a deep level of stillness. It may be a matter of observing the breath, counting the breaths, or experiencing breath as Spirit entering and flowing through us.

If we find it natural to image, our inner seeing may vision flowing light, the person of Jesus, or any image that takes us deep into Being. It may be that we focus on the chakras, or one of them—for example, the heart or the third eye—and gently breathe a mantra into that center.

People who love stories may live into one of the wonderful stories in the Christian gospel because every one of them is a story of transformation. Or perhaps we let an inspirational word or phrase play gently in our hearts and minds. Or simply look at a picture or sculpture that inspires us.

Again it may be the repetition of our sacred word or phrase, the mantra. Especially in conjunction with the breath, the mantra is a powerful gateway to inner experience. Sound, too, is a wonderful way to lead us to this depth. The sound of a bell, a chant, or the waves of the sea.

All of these ways lead us to a great simplicity, to be one before the One. It is good, too, if we wish, to express the experience of meditation—in poetry, art, song or dance. Whichever way is truly expressive for us.

When we talk about meditation, we are in the end talking about a way of being, a way of being mindful in our lives, and a way of being compassionate. We live more fully, and move in the present moment. There is greater attunement to the rhythms of life. Our senses become more alert, too, and our minds clearer.

Perhaps one of the most significant things about meditation is that it is never just for ourselves alone. It is an activity for the universe, and at times we ourselves experience a universal or more-than-personal awareness. When we enter meditation at this level and in union with others, we are powerful agents of healing and peace for the whole world.

When we learn to sit as part of our reverence for life, wisdom and love are given to us.

SUGGESTIONS

1 Find a spot, sit very still and spend some time "blending."
2 Breathe gently into your heart or third eye area. Say a mantra in conjunction with the breath if you wish or simply observe the breath.
3 Sit still and simply notice what happens inside you.
4 Spend half an hour living in the present. Try to be fully attentive to what is happening in each moment.
5 Practise the Jesus prayer. Say the name of Jesus in conjunction with your breathing. Use any variation on the prayer that you wish. Become aware of the breath, then gradually harmonize the mantra with it. Do this for 20 minutes.

CHAPTER 12

THE BREATH WITHIN
THE BREATH

Let us explore the presence of Spirit in our lives.
Jesus described the Spirit as wind that sometimes blows strongly and sometimes barely moves. We do not know where it comes from or where it disappears. It cannot be seen, though we know it is there. We learn that a mighty wind blew on the first Pentecost Sunday. And we remember that when God was revealed to Elijah, it was as a barely perceptible movement of air. The movement of air cleanses and transforms.

Jesus also spoke of Spirit as a fountain of living water springing up into eternal life. We can try to stretch our imaginations to encompass such an image, but perhaps we will never do it. This fountain of living water is in each of us.

I think the phrase "living water" expresses something of the impossibility of really talking about Spirit, because to talk about it, to encase it in words, is to limit it. And Spirit is limitless.

John of the Cross, again attempting to describe the indescribable, wrote of Spirit as "living flame." Living water, living flame. The living flame, the Holy Spirit, does everything in us, cleanses and heals, unites and transforms. John of the Cross, that great disciple of Jesus, wrote of Spirit as Fire, as Breath, and as the gentlest of southern breezes blowing through a scented garden.

Do you have glimpses of Spirit in your life?

My glimpses of Spirit often come when I am entranced by the beauty of something quite small and rarely noticed, or by the beauty of a person in his or her soul. There are glimpses of Spirit for me, too, in the pounding of the sea or the breathless beauty of the moments just before sunrise or just after sunset. Or in the eyes of a child or an old person. Spirit also hovers in mist for me.

Aboriginal Australians know the reality of Spirit in trees, rocks, land and animals. They are our great teachers of Spirit. Other Australians are, too, perhaps especially children or old people or someone handicapped in some way. Indeed, the Celtic ancestors of many Australians were finely attuned to Spirit, and to the sacred everywhere in the universe. I believe, too, that many non-Aboriginal Australians have a spirit-feeling for the land. Every landscape, every seascape has its own Spirit energy. It is as though all matter, in its unique shape and form, is Spirit made visible.

The words we speak for Spirit are often what we might call "feminine" words, not exclusively, of course, for Spirit transcends gender. But when we think of some of the words which describe the spirit of Wisdom in the scriptures, they are words like subtle, permeate, persuasive, gentle, irresistible—words which express something of the nature of feminine energy. It is interesting, too, that in ancient Syriac, Christianity's most ancient language, the word for Spirit was a feminine word, while in the later Latin, the word for Spirit was masculine. Yet, Spirit is most powerfully present in the mutual, equal, loving interaction between masculine and feminine energies both within and between persons. The degree that either one experiences oppression or devaluation by the other is the degree to which Spirit is absent.

For Meister Eckhart, the Holy Spirit is like a rapid river. It is in the flow of this rapid river that true freedom is found. In his sermon on the Holy Spirit, Eckhart focuses on the heart which, to him, is the central and most-to-be-revered part of the human body. For as he says, when the spring of life is born in the heart it takes us into a heavenly awareness and its movement is circular. The heart acts always in this circular way. He surely describes the heart chakra and the nature of Spirit's motion within it. (*Breakthrough*, Serm.26, ed. M. Fox, Image Books, 1980, pp.367-8.)

Sometimes we need to enter a space, internal or external, that is sacred to us, to sit still and let the Spirit heal us. We need often to slow down, to stop, and to listen. To be attuned to the gentleness and delicacy of the little breeze. Only then can we really hear.

So let us do no more encasing in words, but freely open ourselves to the real experience of the Great Spirit—the Breath within the breath, the Living Flame, the still small voice.

SUGGESTIONS

1 Create a sacred space, e.g. draw a mandala on the earth. Sit within it. Open yourself to the healing of the Great Spirit.

2 Feel into your own image(s) of Spirit. Express those images in some way.

3 Ponder "Veni Sancte Spiritus," the sequence for Pentecost. Where do you find yourself in it?

4 Look back over your life at the times you know you have been touched by the Holy Spirit.

5 Sit or walk outside. Let yourself inwardly feel the Spirits of trees, rocks, animals. Notice the times when you feel most connected.

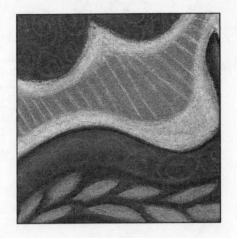

CHAPTER 13

EARTH RECLAIMED

The great Albert Schweitzer spent his life exploring the meaning of a little phrase, "reverence for life." We too will explore something of the meaning of that phrase for our living. For if we explore it sufficiently, and live into it, our lives will be revolutionized.

Some people have been born into awareness that the earth and all that lives is "inspirited." Such people have what we might call a "cosmic awareness." What follows from it turns our ordinary linear thinking inside out. For to know experientially that all of creation shares the one life-flow gives birth to a new consciousness and a new way of living.

We are barely able to glimpse what it would be to live within the sacred, to know each tree, each rock, each person as God-ground. We would know that One Breath breathes through all, and that each being sings itself as cosmic song in harmony with all that is.

So it is quite a serious question when I ask you if you are able to hear the song of a tree, of a koala, or a blade of grass. It is certain that if you sit still long enough and listen, you will.

Moments of cosmic awareness or, as Ken Wilbur calls it, "unity consciousness," happen when we experience ourselves as one with all that is, when we "blend," when we do not experience life as division or separateness but rather as unity and complementarity. It is as though we are part of a vast and glorious symphony in which different musical sounds blend exquisitely. It is at these moments we know God as Simple and

One, as being beyond any Name we might give, and as the All that is in all.

In countries like the U.S. and Australia, this awareness is being glimpsed more and more often as populations attempt to bring listening hearts to a people and a way of being that is as old as the land itself. We allow to open our capacity to wonder, to be childlike, to tell and listen to stories, and to dream.

Time becomes different too. Instead of being marked by a series of events which happen consecutively and being time which moves on or passes, it seems in this new awareness that it is time that stands still and holds all that is in that stillness. It is time where "all is always now." It is the timeless time in which myth is woven.

"Reverence for life" changes our way of relating to the earth. It is a way which nurtures and does not exploit. It knows that if we hurt the earth we hurt our own souls, for we are one with her. It knows that the fineness of her balance is a miracle, and seeks to respect and live in harmony with her. It knows, too, that she has suffered too much.

There is a way of being that is "reverence for life." It is called "mindfulness." It means that in whatever we do, we are wholly present and aware in the present. It means we take as much time as we need to do everything we do. It means we touch reverently, we listen deeply, and we act with care and love. No part of us is absent to *this* moment, *this* task, *this* person.

When we meditate, too, we move into this "being" awareness. We sit still, we become centered, we "let go and let be." Gradually we find that instead of the experience of "I am breathing," it is one of "I am being breathed." Our personal, often ego-centered, awareness has given way to a transcendent cosmic awareness.

Two people may see a beautiful flower. One may pick it, examine it, count its petals, even pull it to pieces to see how it fits together. The other may simply delight in its beauty and come to know it from within. Two people may climb a mountain. One may experience reaching the summit as conquering the mountain, the other as befriending it.

We spoke earlier of the inner child. Let us spend time with the child again, especially in his or her capacity to be in awe, to wonder, to sit totally absorbed, to delight. Let us sit so still, with our souls so gentled that we hear and sing the song of the earth.

SUGGESTIONS

1 Practise blending with your surroundings.
2 Sit on the earth and feel its life.
3 Let a tree tell you its story.
4 Walk blindfolded among some trees.
5 Do a meditation of the senses. Spend about five minutes experiencing each of the senses, then five minutes experiencing them all together. Notice what happens.
6 Can you perceive the fields of energy surrounding living things? Relax your eyes and look in an unfocused way. What do you see? Draw it.

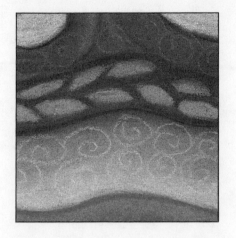

CHAPTER 14

JOURNEY ON

One of the great patterns of the human experience is the journey. Often, when we reflect on our own life, we think of it as a journey, sometimes rough, sometimes gentle, sometimes exploring, sometimes discovering. From time immemorial the records of humanity's striving have been in the form of a journey. We may reflect on and enter experientially our own journey.

Journeys have beginnings and endings, and so, with the inner journey implicit in the pages of this book, in this chapter we come to an ending. But every ending is also a beginning. Today we begin, consciously and gratefully, the journey of the rest of our lives.

Let us reflect on some of the patterns of journey, and, within that, the unique pattern of our own story. Let that pattern reveal itself to us. Our stories are somewhat like a woven tapestry, of greater and lesser motifs, of blended colors, of fine or coarse texture.

Is your pattern one of leaving home and returning home? Is it one of going down into deep water or into the underworld and coming up again? Is it one of growing from a tiny seed into a great tree or beautiful flower? Or perhaps you are a climber of mountains or on quest in search of treasure? Let yourself *feel into* the particular nature of your journey.

We have most probably met some of the great journeyers—Odysseus, whose story depicts his return home as king to his own island of Ithaca; Innana, the goddess who descended into the underworld to be reborn; Jonah, who spent three days and nights in the belly of the whale; Teresa of Avila, who journeyed to the center of her interior castle; or the Buddha, whose journey was to awakening or enlightenment.

There is, too, the great paradigm journey for Christians, that is, the journey of Jesus. One of the strong motifs of Jesus' journey is that of leaving home and returning home. Another is that of rejection by those for whom he gave his life. Or yet another, his sense of destiny as he set his face towards Jerusalem. There is, too, the pattern of his descent into the earth and his rising from it. The whole of Luke's gospel, for instance, is couched in the pattern of journey.

In allowing our myth as sacred story to reveal itself to us, we may like to ponder some questions and to make jottings, as connections into our story come to us. We may ask ourselves, for instance, what we know of our ancestry. Which of the human patterns of our ancestors are being carried and lived by us? Do we have a sense of the different milestones or stepping stones that are the building blocks of the patterns in our personal story? As we look back along the road of our life, what events do we remember? Is there a symbol or symbolic pattern that can hold the ongoingness and depth of our story? Do we prefer to tell our story as poetry, dance or song, or as an historical reconstruction? How do we perceive the meaning of life for us?

Keeping a journal is a good way of tuning in to our story. The journal is our own special book. We write in it what matters to us in the way we like to write. As many journal-keepers experience, the journal becomes their friend. Many years ago, Ed Farrell wrote a book in which he likened the keeping of a journal to the journey to Emmaus. When we keep a journal our eyes are opened, we move from darkness to light as the disciples did, and from alienation to connection.

We will complete the contemplation of our journey by spending time entering into our Emmaus story, and finding ourselves where we belong in it.

Like the disciples, we have our times of alienation, aloneness, lostness. It is good not to resist the pain of this state as it is for us. Every experience we have is a "word" to be listened to. Sometimes we, too, become absorbed in our desolation, and, like the disciples, cannot seem to lift ourselves out of its heaviness to notice what or who is around us. But something happened in the disciples as this stranger walked beside them. He seemed to have an inner understanding of the scriptures too. Gradually, almost unaware to themselves, the hearts of the disciples changed. Their heavy dark hearts began to lighten and even to burn.

We find this journey to Emmaus took a day. They left Jerusalem in the morning and arrived at Emmaus in the evening. Often the sun's rising is the journey's beginning, and its setting its ending. And so, as evening came, the disciples and their fellow-traveller arrived home. With the typical hospitality of the East, they invited Jesus to their home. And only then, after they had journeyed, after their hearts had been transformed, after they had come home and invited Jesus into that home, did he reveal himself to them. They recognized him in that familiar gesture which most of us do sometime every day, the breaking of bread. And then he disappeared.

The story of Emmaus is a story of enlightenment and of transformation of heart. Every time we live into it, it happens in us.

What is your story? How does it want to tell itself? What are the weaving threads of your life journey? Let us move into the conscious living of your story, to become aware of its mythological patterns, the dancing together of its symbols, the patterns and colors of its feelings, the gift of memories given to be woven in and let go.

Let's be weavers of stories today—ours. And finally, let us return to the very first day when we let some of our journey-questions move in our hearts. What is happening in our journey now? When did it begin? How is it unfolding? How do I want to tell it? With whom do I want to share it?

And so we journey on...

SUGGESTIONS

1 **Draw a map of your soul country. Let significant formative events in your journey be trees, valleys, mountains, cities, etc.**
2 **Live into your stepping stones again, perhaps in a different way than you have before. Let those**

significant events come to you when you look back on
your journey to this point. Feel the stepping stones as
a continuum and also give thoughtful attention to
each of them. What patterns do they reveal? Can you
see the interplay of opposites in them? What is the
hidden face of each stepping stone? Let each one be a
chapter heading in your story.

3 Walk among your symbols and let them speak your
story. Which symbol or symbolic pattern reflects your
truth? Spend time living into each of your symbols.
Become the symbols.

4 Let memories come and jot them down. Find some
childhood photos.

5 Look back at your statement beginning with the
words "The meaning of my life is..." Is it right for
now?

6 Let your sacred story tell itself to you. When are the
light times and when are the dark times in your story?
Relive both. What are its patterns?

7 Share your story.

8 Write your story in a special book—as poetry, as art,
as history, as myth.

SUGGESTED
READING LIST

Abrams, Jeremiah (ed.). *Reclaiming the Inner Child.* Mandala, 1991.

Brennan, Barbara Ann. *Hands of Light.* Bantam, 1987.

Estes, Clarissa Pinkola. *Women Who Run With Wolves.* Rider, 1992.

Hillman, James. *A Blue Fire.* Harper & Row, 1989.

Johnson, Robert. *Inner Work.* Harper & Row, 1986.

Le Guin, Ursula. *Earthsea Trilogy.* Puffin, 1974.

McMurray, Madeline. *Illuminations: The Healing Image.* Berkeley, California: Wingbow Press, 1988.

Sanford, John A. *The Invisible Partners.* Paulist Press, 1980.

Stevens, Edward. *Spiritual Technologies: A User's Manual.* Paulist Press, 1990.

Woodman, Marion. *The Pregnant Virgin.* Inner City Books, 1985.